Our
GOVERNMENT
LEADERS

MEMBER OF CONGRESS

by Jacqueline Laks Gorman

Reading consultant: Susan Nations, M.Ed., author/literacy coach/consultant

WR WEEKLY READER
EARLY LEARNING LIBRARY

Please visit our web site at: **www.earlyliteracy.cc**
For a free color catalog describing Weekly Reader® Early Learning Library's
list of high-quality books, call 1-877-445-5824 (USA) or 1-800-387-3178 (Canada).
Weekly Reader® Early Learning Library's fax: (414) 336-0164.

Library of Congress Cataloging-in-Publication Data

Gorman, Jacqueline Laks, 1955-
     Member of Congress / by Jacqueline Laks Gorman.
          p. cm. — (Our government leaders)
     Includes bibliographical references and index.
     ISBN 0-8368-4570-6 (lib. bdg.)
     ISBN 0-8368-4577-3 (softcover)
     1. United States. Congress—Juvenile literature.   2. Legislators—United States—
Juvenile literature.   I. Title. II. Series.
     JK1025.G67   2005
     328.73—dc22   2004043113

This edition first published in 2005 by
Weekly Reader® Early Learning Library
330 West Olive Street, Suite 100
Milwaukee, WI 53212 USA

Editor: Barbara Kiely Miller
Cover and layout design: Melissa Valuch
Photo research: Diane Laska-Swanke

Photo credits: Cover, title, © Paul J. Richards/AFP/Getty Images; p. 5 © Library of Congress/Getty
Images; p. 6 © Stephen Jaffe/AFP/Getty Images; p. 7 © Nancy Carter/North Wind Picture Archives;
p. 9 © Brendan Smialowski/Getty Images; pp. 10, 13 © Alex Wong/Getty Images; p. 11 © Paul J. Richards/
AFP/Getty Images; p. 12 © Gjon Mili/Time & Life Pictures/Getty Images; p. 15 © Ken Lambert/Washington
Times via Getty Images; p. 16 © Kean Collection/Getty Images; p. 17 © B. Kelley/Time & Life Pictures/
Getty Images; p. 19 © Stock Montage, Inc.; p. 20 © New York Times Co./Getty Images; p. 21 © Pool
Photo/Getty Images

Printed in the United States of America

1 2 3 4 5 6 7 8 9 09 08 07 06 05

Cover Photo: Dianne Feinstein has been a senator from California since 1992. She
             is shown speaking at the Democratic National Convention in 2004.

TABLE OF CONTENTS

Chapter 1: Who Are Members of Congress? . . .4

Chapter 2: What Do Members of Congress Do? . . .8

Chapter 3: How Do People Get to Be

Members of Congress? 14

Chapter 4: Famous Members of Congress . .18

Glossary 22

For More Information 23

Index 24

CHAPTER 1

Who Are Members of Congress?

Congress has two parts. One part is the Senate. The other is the House of Representatives. Men and women who serve in the Senate are called **senators**. Men and women in the House are called **representatives**. They are all members of Congress.

There are one hundred senators. Each of the fifty states has two senators. Each senator serves a **term**, or period in office, of six years. Each senator represents his or her entire state.

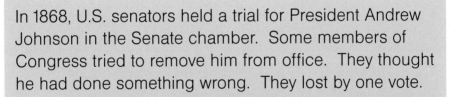

In 1868, U.S. senators held a trial for President Andrew Johnson in the Senate chamber. Some members of Congress tried to remove him from office. They thought he had done something wrong. They lost by one vote.

In January 2004, President George W. Bush spoke to all the members of Congress. He spoke to them in the House chamber.

There are 435 representatives. Each state has at least one representative. States that have more people have more representatives. A representative's term is two years long. He or she does not represent all the people in his or her state. A representative only serves people in part of the state.

Members of Congress work in Washington, D.C. They meet in the U.S. Capitol building. They have offices there and in other buildings nearby. Members of Congress live in two places. Part of the time, they live in Washington, D.C. They live in their home states the rest of the time. They also have small offices in their home states.

© Nancy Carter/North Wind Picture Archives

Members of Congress meet in the U.S. Capitol building. The Capitol is in Washington, D.C.

CHAPTER 2

What Do Members of Congress Do?

The main job of Congress is to pass laws. An idea for a new law is called a bill. First, a senator or representative suggests the bill. Then the Senate and the House each studies the bill separately.

A group of senators or representatives meets to talk about the bill. This group is called a **committee**. The committee holds **hearings**, or public meetings, on the bill. The committee members vote on the bill. If most of them think it is a good bill, it is sent to the rest of the Senate and the House members.

Committees hold public hearings on important issues. A Senate hearing heard facts about the terrorist attacks of September 11, 2001.

Senators John McCain (*left*) of Arizona and Russ Feingold (*right*) of Wisconsin worked together on a bill to make campaigns more fair.

The Senate and the House vote on the bill. For a bill to pass, a majority vote is needed. The bill must pass both the Senate and the House. If it passes, it is sent to the president. If the president likes the bill, he signs it. Then it becomes a law.

If the president does not like the bill, he does not have to sign it. When he does not sign a bill, it is called a **veto**. However, a veto is not the end of the bill. Congress can still pass it. To do this, two-thirds of the members of Congress must vote for the bill. Then it becomes a law.

In 1993, Congress passed a bill about trading with Mexico and Canada. The leaders of the Senate and the House watched as President Bill Clinton signed the bill.

In 1973, a Senate committee held hearings to see whether people in government had done something wrong.

Members of Congress also hold hearings on important issues. They study problems in the country. They look for ways to solve the problems.

Senators vote for people the president chooses for certain jobs in the government. They must also approve agreements with other countries.

Members of Congress also help the people in their home states or districts. They make sure the government helps people. They also make sure the people's ideas are heard. Members of Congress visit their home states often. When they visit, they talk to the people. They find out what the people whom they represent need.

The president chooses people for some government jobs. They must come to Senate hearings to be approved.

CHAPTER 3

How Do People Get to Be Members of Congress?

Senators must be at least thirty years old. They must have been citizens of the United States for at least nine years. They must live in their home state.

Representatives must be at least twenty-five years old. They must have been citizens for at least seven years. They must live in their home district.

Members of the House of Representatives have to run for election every two years. Senators must run every six years. Members of Congress can run for office as many times as they want. Some people have been in Congress for many years.

New members of the House of Representatives meet in Washington, D.C., after they are elected.

People who want to be members of Congress have to campaign. They travel around their state or district. They talk to voters. They give speeches. They have debates in which they share their ideas.

In 1858, Abraham Lincoln (*left*) and Stephen Douglas (*right*) ran for the Senate from Illinois. They had several debates to share their ideas.

Incumbents are people who are already in an office. They have a good chance of being elected again. Sometimes no one wants to run against them. In November, people vote for the candidate they like best. The person with the most votes is elected.

Strom Thurmond of South Carolina served in the Senate longer than anyone else — from 1954 until 2003.

CHAPTER 4

Famous Members of Congress

Many members of Congress have done great things for the nation. Many served in Congress for years and years. In the 1800s, John C. Calhoun and Henry Clay were leaders of Congress. They both worked hard for the people.

John Quincy Adams was president from 1825 to 1829. Before he became president, Adams was a senator. After he was president, he became a representative for eighteen years. He is the only president to go to the House after being president. Adams fought hard against slavery when he was a member of Congress.

After he was president, John Quincy Adams served in the House of Representatives from 1830 to 1848.

Jeannette Rankin was the first woman ever elected to Congress.

Jeannette Rankin came from Montana. In 1916, she became the first woman elected to Congress. She served one term in the House. She served another term in the 1940s. Since then, many other women have been elected to Congress.

Hillary Rodham Clinton is married to former President Bill Clinton. She was the first lady of the United States from 1993 to 2001. She ran for the Senate in 2000 and won. She is the only woman who has been first lady and also elected to office herself.

Senator Hillary Rodham Clinton of New York (*right*) and other members of Congress work together to make the country stronger.

Glossary

bill — an idea for a new law that Congress is considering voting on

campaign — to take part in organized activities in order to get elected

citizens — official members of a country who are given certain rights, such as voting and freedom of speech. Citizens also have duties, such as paying taxes.

debates — discussions of people's different ideas and why they are for or against something

district — a specific area in a state that a member of the House of Representatives serves and represents. Districts are determined by population.

incumbents — people who hold a political office

term — a specific period of time that a person serves in office

veto — the president's rejection of a bill passed by Congress

For More Information

Books

D Is for Democracy: A Citizen's Alphabet. Elissa Grodin (Thomson Gale)

The U.S. Congress. Let's See Library: Our Nation (series). Patricia J. Murphy (Compass Point Books)

The U.S. House of Representatives. First Facts: Our Government (series). Muriel L. Dubois (Capstone Press)

The U.S. Senate. First Facts: Our Government (series). Muriel L. Dubois (Capstone Press)

Web Sites

Congress for Kids
www.congressforkids.net
How the branches of Congress work and what they do

Kids in the House–Office of the Clerk, U.S. House of Representatives
clerkkids.house.gov
Take a trip around the Capitol building and learn about Congress and how laws are made

Index

Adams, John Quincy 19
Calhoun, John C. 18
capitol building 7
Clinton, Hillary Rodham 21
Douglas, Stephen 16
duties 8, 9, 10, 11, 12, 13
elections 15, 16, 17
Feingold, Russ 10
Feinstein, Dianne 2
hearings 9, 12, 13
Johnson, Andrew 5

laws 8, 9, 10, 11
Lincoln, Abraham 16
McCain, John 10
Rankin, Jeannette 20
requirements 14
representatives 4, 6, 14, 15
senators 4, 5, 12, 14, 15
terms 5, 6, 15
Thurmond, Strom 17
women in Congress 2, 20, 21

About the Author

Jacqueline Laks Gorman is a writer and editor. She grew up in New York City. She has worked on many kinds of books and has written several children's series. She lives with her husband, David, and children, Colin and Caitlin, in DeKalb, Illinois. She always votes in every election.